Published by
North Atlantic Books
Berkeley, California

Cover art and design by Ruby Roth
Book design by Ruby Roth

Printed in the United States of America

That's Why We Don't Eat Animals: A Book About Vegans, Vegetarians, and All Living Things is sponsored and published by the Society for the Study of Native Arts and Sciences (dba North Atlantic Books), an educational nonprofit based in Berkeley, California, that collaborates with partners to develop cross-cultural perspectives, nurture holistic views of art, science, the humanities, and healing, and seed personal and global transformation by publishing work on the relationship of body, spirit, and nature.

North Atlantic Books' publications are available through most bookstores. For further information, visit our website at www.northatlanticbooks.com or call 800-733-3000.

Library of Congress Cataloging-in-Publication Data
Roth, Ruby.
  That's why we don't eat animals / written and illustrated by Ruby Roth.
    p. cm.
  ISBN 978-1-55643-785-4
  1. Vegetarianism—Juvenile literature. 2. Vegetarianism—Moral and
ethical aspects—Juvenile literature. I. Title.
  TX392.R74 2009
  641.5'636—dc22
                                    2008055482

Printed and bound by QuaLibre/CG Book Printers, June 2016, in the United States. Job #205559.

6 7 8 9 10 QuaLibre/CG Book Printers 19 18 17 16

Printed on recycled paper

That's Why We Don't Eat Animals

A Book About Vegans, Vegetarians, and All Living Things

Written and Illustrated
by Ruby Roth

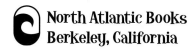

North Atlantic Books
Berkeley, California

A flower will push through a crack in the sidewalk in order to feel the sun. A penguin will march thousands of miles to find food for her babies. The thunderous roar of a lion protects his family from danger near and far. Whether it has gills, wings, whiskers, or roots, every living being shares the will to live and grow.

We are all *earthlings.*

While some animals are protected by laws or born into loving homes, others live painful and lonely lives on factory farms where hundreds or thousands of animals are raised for meat and dairy. But they too live and breathe. They too have feelings and families.

People throughout history have chosen not to eat these fellow earthlings. *Vegetarians* are people who don't eat animals. *Vegans* are people who don't eat animals or anything that comes from an animal (like eggs, milk, or butter). We strive for a world where every earthling has the right to live and grow.

That's why we don't eat animals.

Pets

Pets are members of our family. They nuzzle us and we play together; we pet them and we both feel calm. Their love is so powerful that it can even help us heal. They can tell when we feel lonely, just as we can tell when they want dinner. We know each other by heart.

All animals deserve the care and protection we give our pets.

Animal Families

Just like we do, many baby animals stay close to their parents long after they're born. Our families warm, protect, and comfort us, preparing us for the great big world.

On factory farms, there are no animal families. With no mama in sight, these babies live without a sense of family or safety. Animals belong in families, packs, herds, and flocks.

Chickens

A hen lays eggs that will one day be her babies. In a carefully planned nest, she and her chicks coo to each other before the eggs even hatch. Roosters keep watch, and older chicks play chase, tag, and hide-and-seek.

Crammed into cages on factory farms,
chickens have no room to live. There's no land
to explore, no dust to bathe in, no dirt to peck,
poke, or scratch. There's barely space to
spread their wings.

Turkeys

When a turkey dances, jumps, gobbles, and flaps its wings, others join in celebration. Turkeys also mourn together, sharing each other's sadness. They're so sensitive that they even blush. Their snoods change color depending on their mood.

When the moon rises, wild turkeys fly to the treetops to roost for the night, gathering together beneath each other's wings.
A factory-farm turkey will never get to use her wings at all. Turkeys raised for meat are fattened until they become too heavy to fly.

Quail

No bigger than bumblebees, newborn quail start walking as soon as they pop out of their eggs. Quail are fierce parents who will do anything to protect their babies. But they can't protect them from hunters.

On many farms, quail are raised just for gaming, which means they're hunted for fun. Is that fair to a family of quail?

Ducks & Geese

Every winter, ducks and geese journey across the Earth to lands where their babies will be warm. They fly through the skies for days and months, crossing over states and even entire countries.

But factory-farm ducks and geese are caged behind bars and force-fed to make them fat. The skies above them are endless, but these birds will never fly.

Birds raised for meat, called *poultry*, are just like the birds we see outside our windows. But they don't receive the same love and protection that free birds do. Crowded together, they can't follow their instincts, so they grow sick and scared. Soon they begin to lose their feathers.

Birds are meant to use their wings to fly, their beaks to feed, and their feathers to flock together.

Pigs

It should be a compliment to be called a pig!
Pigs are some of the smartest, cleanest, and
most sensitive animals on planet Earth.

Free pigs live with their families and friends.
Snorting and whistling, they recognize each other's
voices from far away. They root for food, wrestle, and
play ball in the sun, but they don't sweat like we do to
keep cool when they play. They take mud baths to cool
off instead. A muddy pig is a wise pig.

A factory-farm pig may spend her whole life alone, fattened in a pen so tiny that she won't even be able to turn around. A free pig never poops where she eats or sleeps, but on a factory farm she has no choice.

Pigs need the sight, sound, and touch of one another. Sometimes they snuggle so close that it's hard to get them apart.

Love is part of their nature.

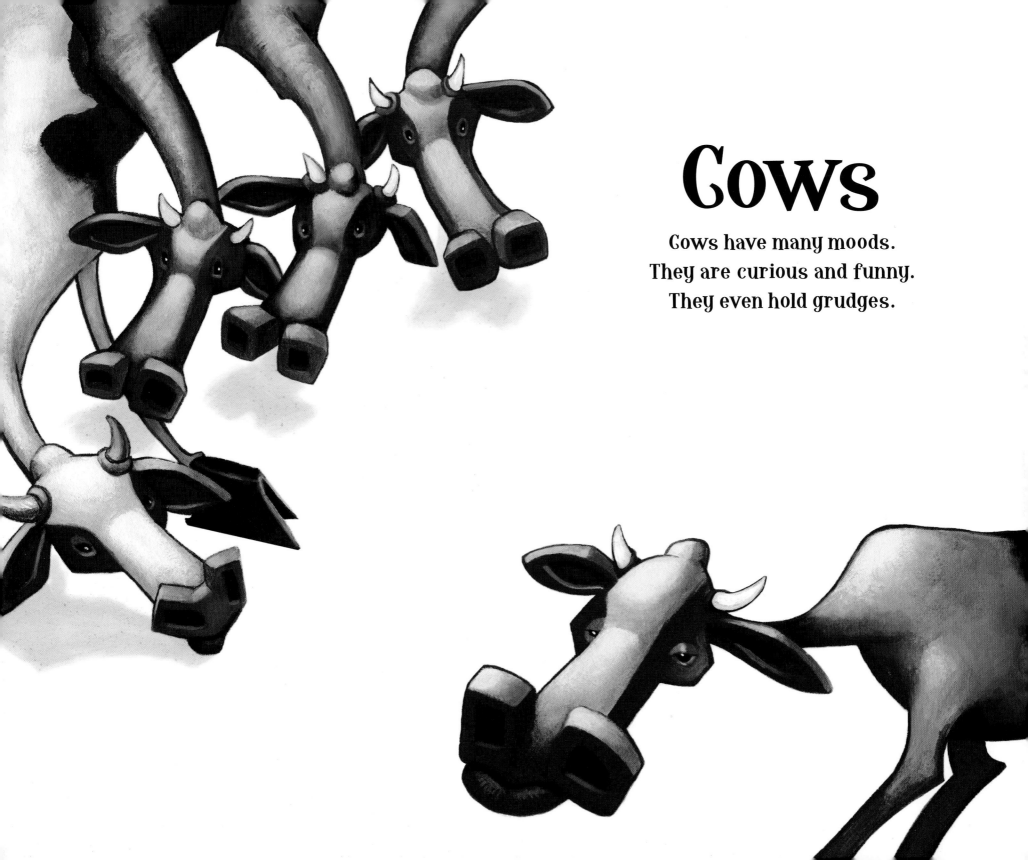

Cows

Cows have many moods.
They are curious and funny.
They even hold grudges.

Proud cows show off, best friends take walks together, and calves play follow-the-leader. Herds behave like big families, staying close to each other and even mooing together until a wandering cow finds her way back home.

On factory farms, cows are unable to be with their families, stretch, or chew fresh grass under the sun. They're fed corn, which fattens them and gives them stomachaches and gas.

Cattle farms waste precious water and make pollution that leaks into the ocean and sky. Growing vegetables instead of raising animals could save our planet's oceans, air, and sea life. And the food and water we'd save could feed more hungry people all over the world.

The Ocean

Beyond our shores exists another world, an underwater kingdom ruled by ancient and majestic beings. Wise blue whales circle the depths of Earth's oceans. Their gigantic hearts, each the size of a small car, boom as they glide through the waters.

Giant turtles are the great protectors of the ocean's sea grass beds. They keep them healthy for all sea life.

Dolphins are brilliant creatures, one of the smartest species on Earth. They speak to each other in a language of clicks and chatter.

Although humans live on land, the foods we eat and the waste we make affect the ocean and everything in it.

Fish

Fish have extraordinary senses. They have quick instincts and delicate nerves. Their bodies can feel nearby fish, food, and objects—without even touching them.

Fish are part of the ocean's ecosystem, a giant family of plants and animals. Each group needs the others to keep the whole family alive and healthy.

Every year, fishing nets tangle and crush billions of fish and thousands of sea turtles, whales, dolphins, and sharks that are part of the ecosystem.

Earth's oceans and rivers are truly being emptied of fish and sea mammals. Can you imagine an ocean with no fish?

The Rainforest

Home to some of our world's most
magnificent plants, animals, foods, and
medicines, the rainforest is the most
powerful and valuable natural
resource on Earth.

Forests help keep the air clean and
the Earth from getting too warm.
The Amazon Rainforest, one of the
world's largest, has been called
"the lungs of the planet."

Endangered Species

Today, ancient forests once lush and wild are
slashed and burned down to make room for cattle
farms. The fires create pollution and leave animals
with no food or shelter. Plants, animals, foods, and
medicines are wiped out forever.

Plants and animals around the world are in danger of being lost. Many are already gone. As earthlings, we depend on each other. We may think we are separate, but we are all woven into the same web of life. When we destroy the rainforest and the animals there, we are destroying ourselves.

We must consider how the foods
we eat affect the planet.

In many cultures around the world, there is a saying that tells us "you are what you eat." When we eat natural foods, we soak up the goodness of the sun, the Earth, the roots, and the trees. We grow to be healthier and pay more attention to our choices.

While the power of nature can move
mountains and make rainbows, the power we
have as humans is boundless too. Every day,
we have the freedom to change our lives. In
fact, when we treat animals respectfully, we
practice world peace.

That's why we don't eat animals.

What Else Can We Do?

Read books on animals, veganism, vegetarianism, and raw foods.

Discover new vegetarian and vegan foods.

Write a school report on veganism and vegetarianism.

Look up raw, vegan, and vegetarian recipes and products on the internet with your parents.

Buy clothes, shoes, belts, and bags that are not made from fur, leather, or other animal skins.

Look for foods that are grown "sustainably." This means that the crops are grown in a way that nourishes the Earth, animals, and environment, instead of depleting them.

Look for products and foods that are labeled with cruelty-free logos like this one:

cruelty-free

Celebrate Thanksgiving with a vegan feast.

If you want a pet, adopt one from the pound instead of buying from a store or breeder. Keep them healthy and make sure to spay or neuter your pets to avoid unwanted animals.

Feed your pets vegetarian pet food.

Join an organization that helps the Earth, animals, and the environment.

Recycle and re-use.